Artful Blessings

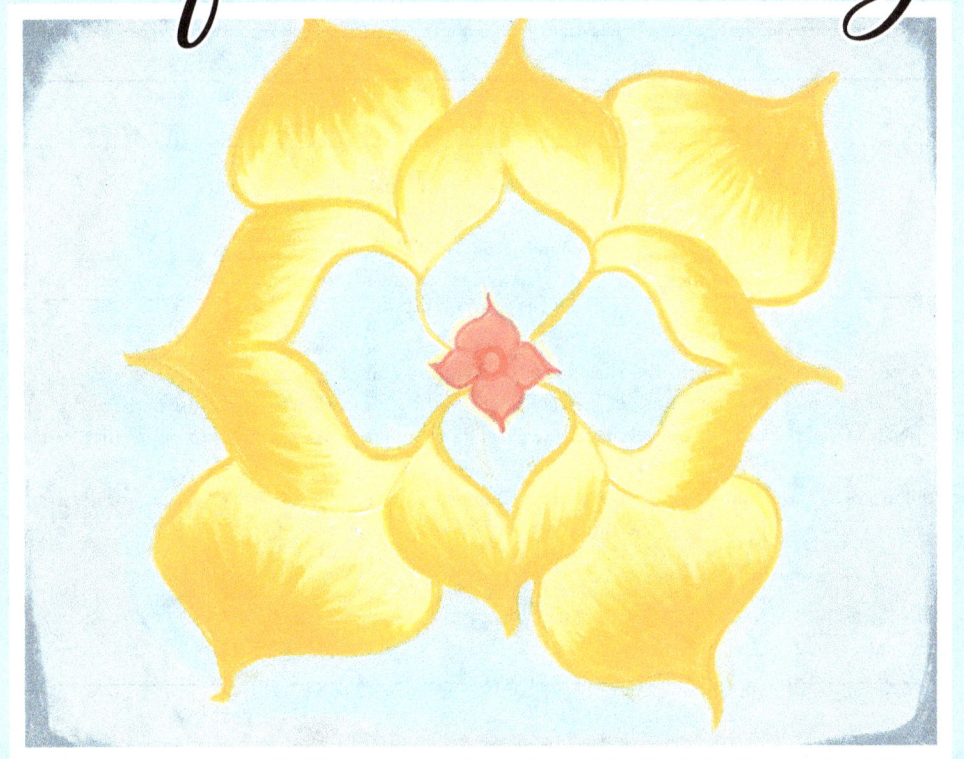

written and illustrated by

Lidia L. Santiago

Balboa Press books may be ordered through booksellers or by contacting:

Balboa Press
A Division of Hay House
1663 Liberty Drive
Bloomington, IN 47403
www.balboapress.com
1 (877) 407-4847

Because of the dynamic nature of the Internet, any web addresses or links contained in this book may have changed since publication and may no longer be valid. The views expressed in this work are solely those of the author and do not necessarily reflect the views of the publisher, and the publisher hereby disclaims any responsibility for them.

Any people depicted in stock imagery provided by Thinkstock are models, and such images are being used for illustrative purposes only. Certain stock imagery © Thinkstock.

ISBN: 978-1-4525-8970-1 (sc)
ISBN: 978-1-4525-8971-8 (e)

Printed in the United States of America.

Balboa Press rev. date: 1/8/2014

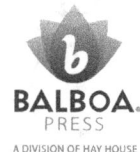

BALBOA
PRESS
A DIVISION OF HAY HOUSE

I would like to thank all of the Angels that helped make this little art book possible, in Heaven and on Earth, with all my heart, I thank you.

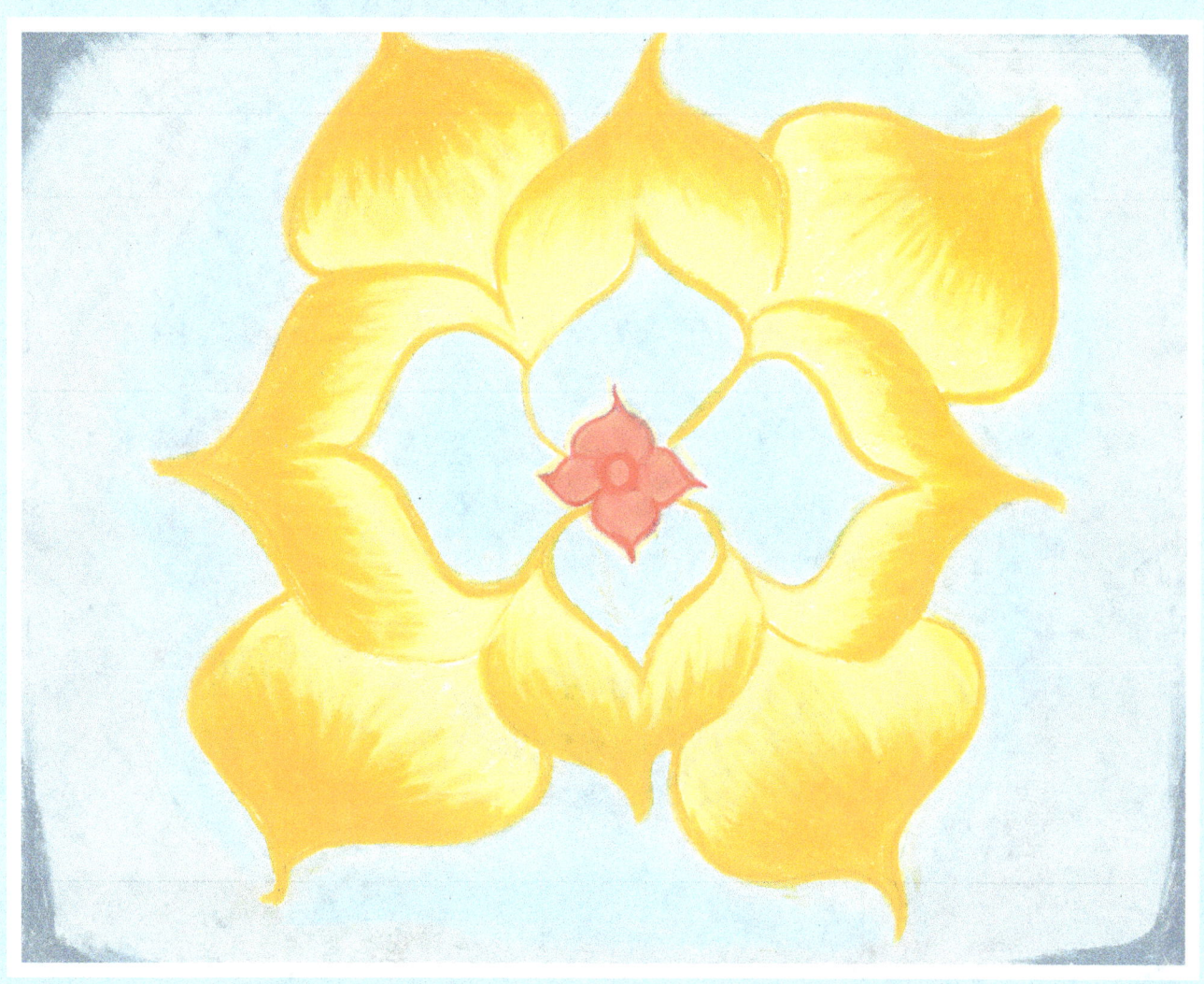

Blessings of Illumination

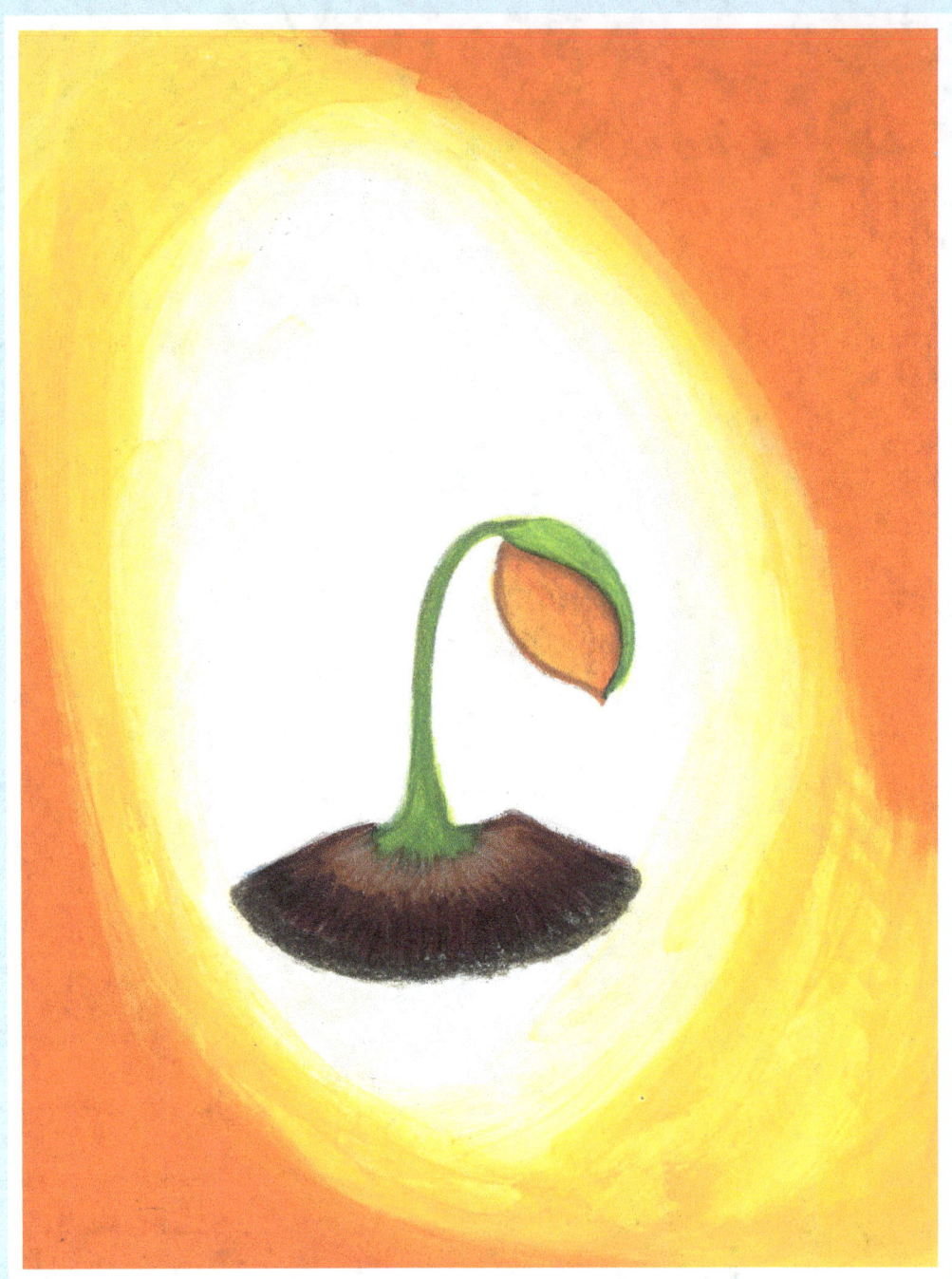

Blessings of Hope

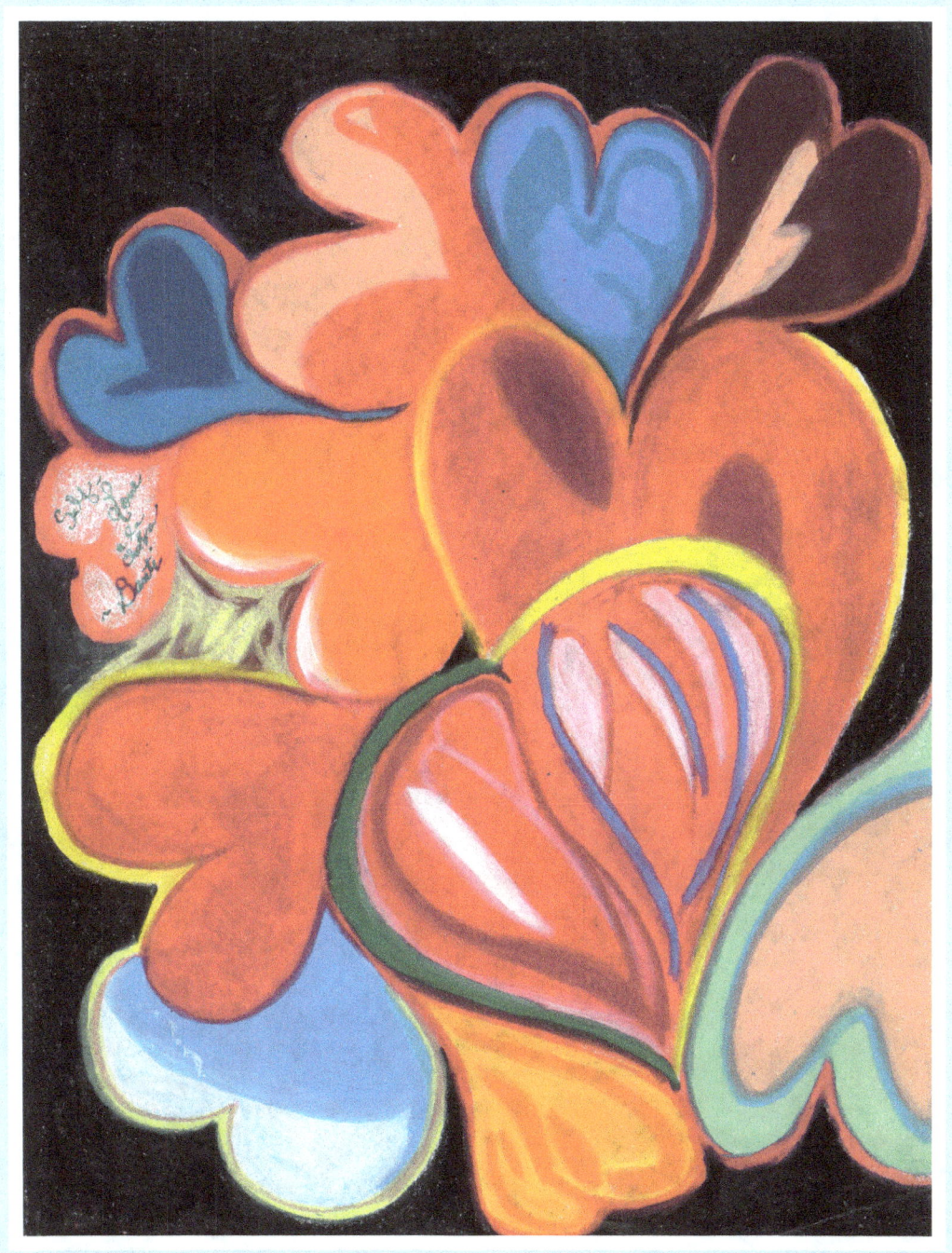

Blessing of Self Love

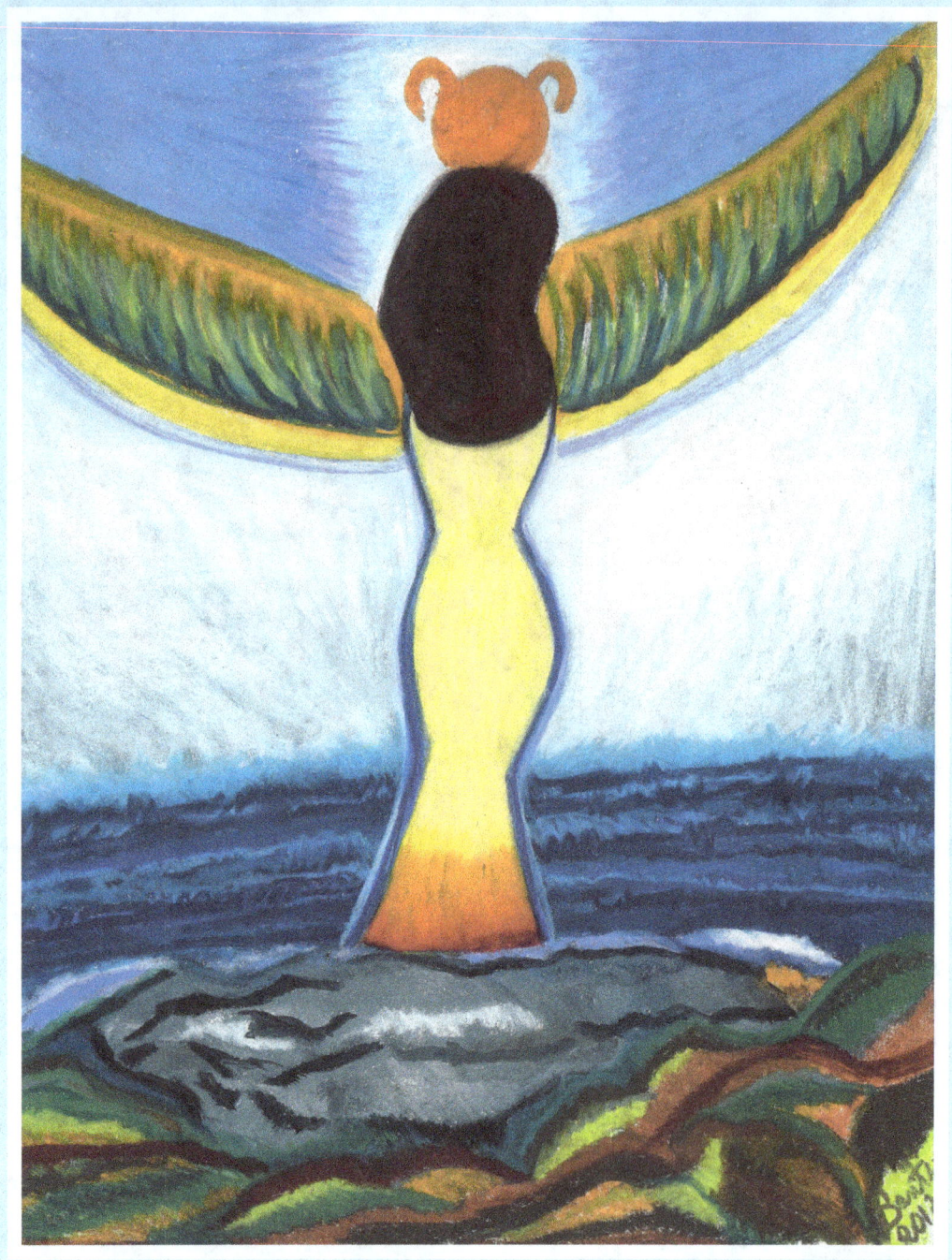

Blessings of Empowerment

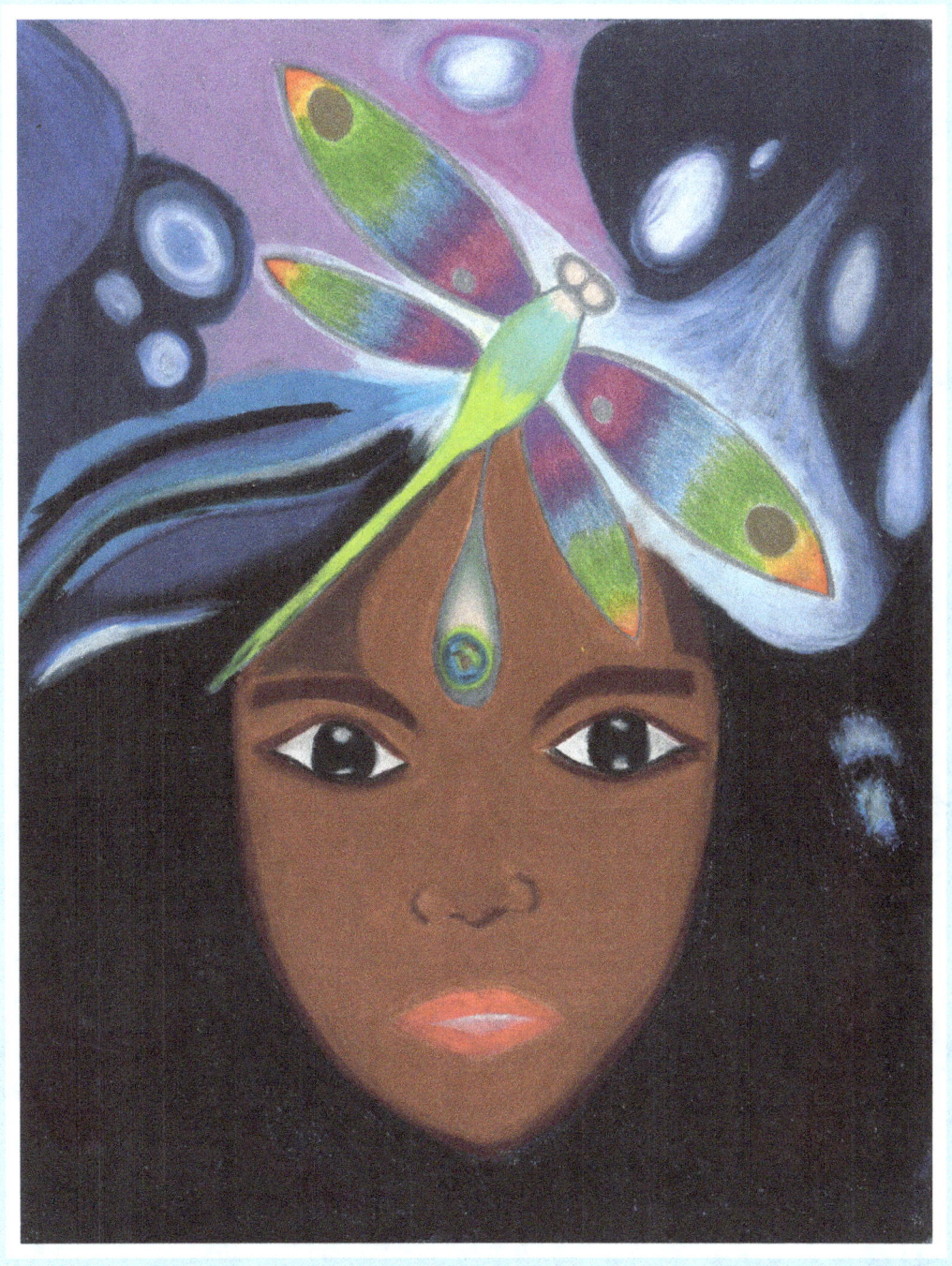

Blessings of Transformation

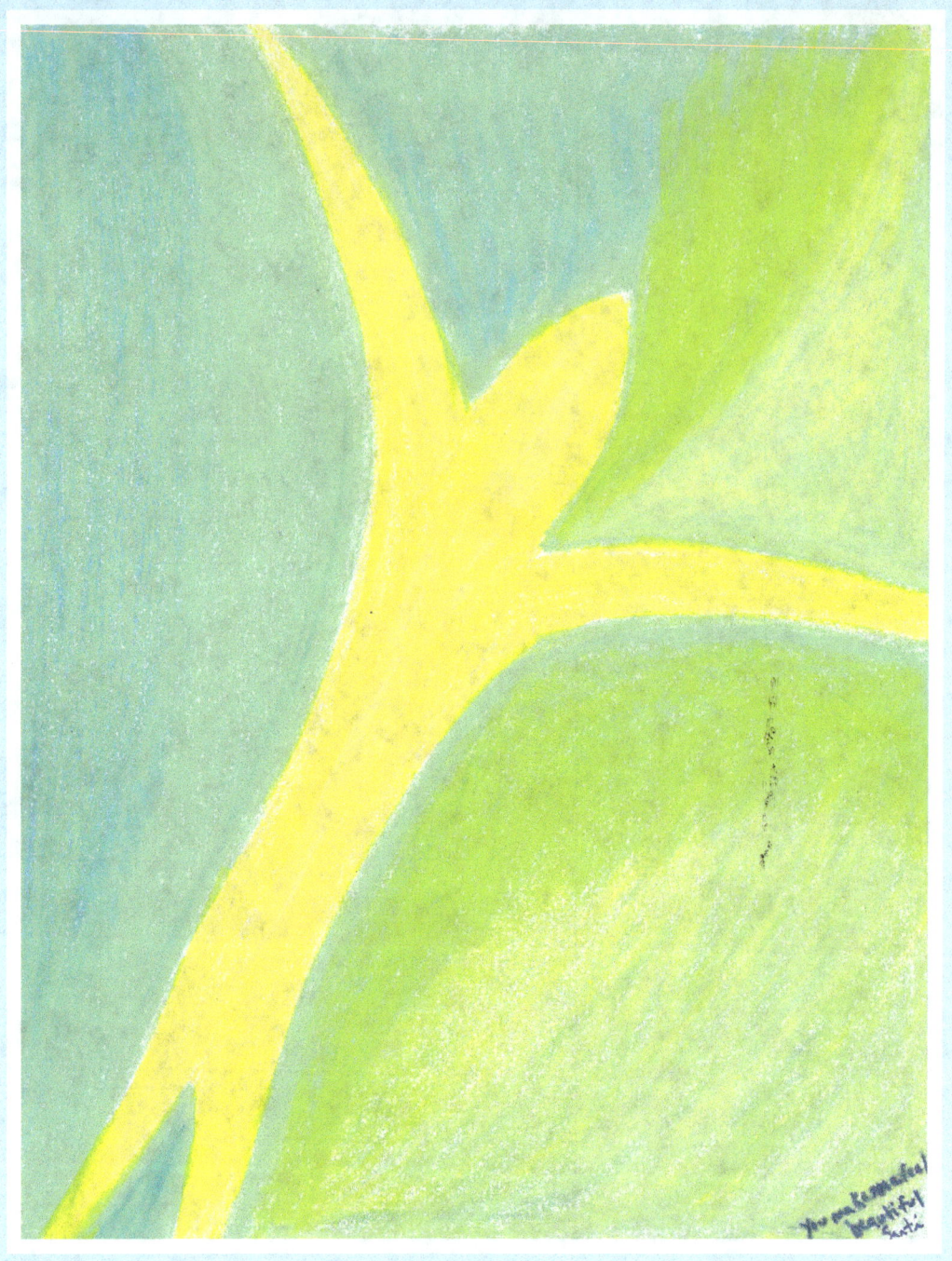

Blessings of Joy

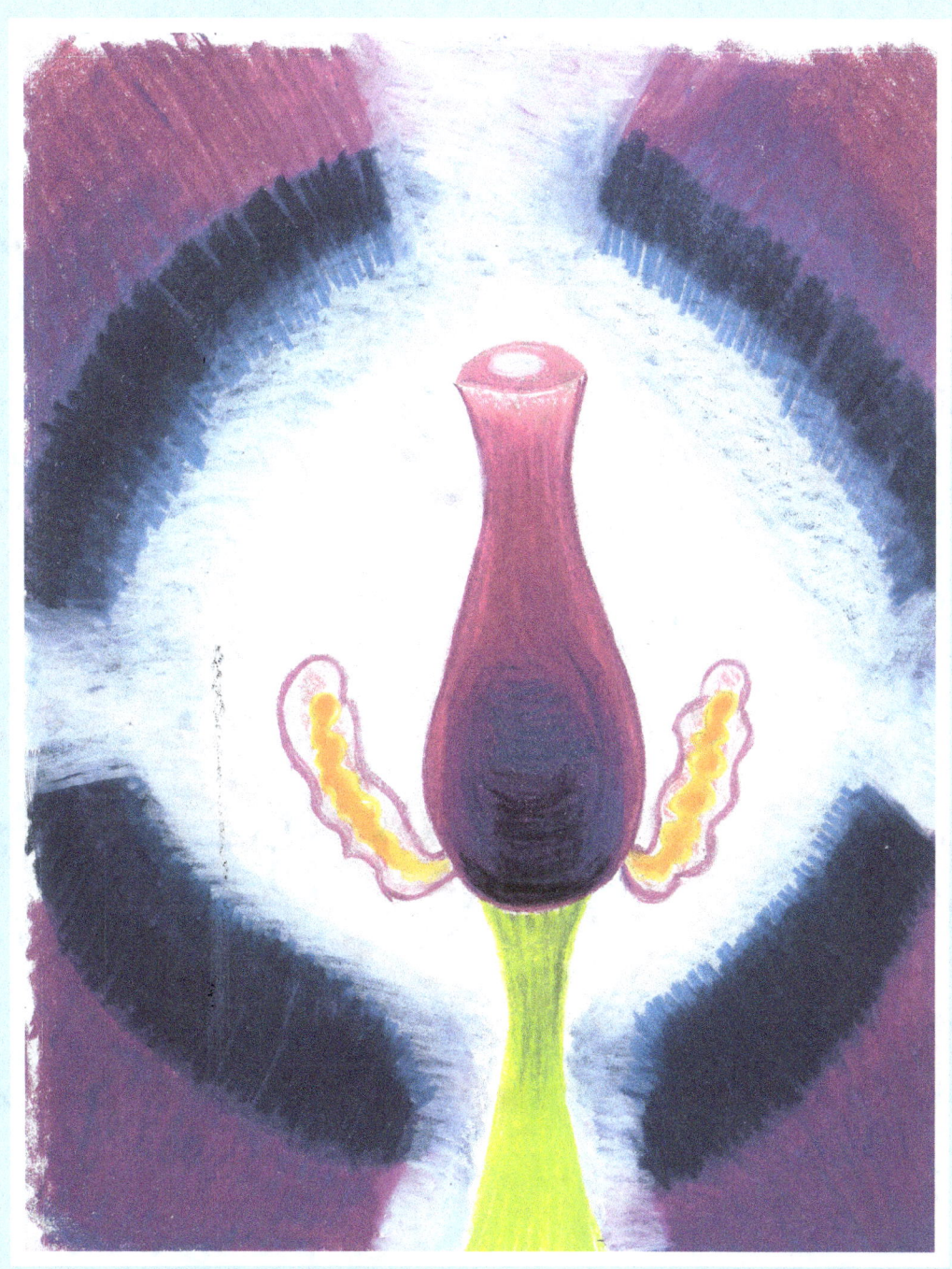

Blessings of Fertility

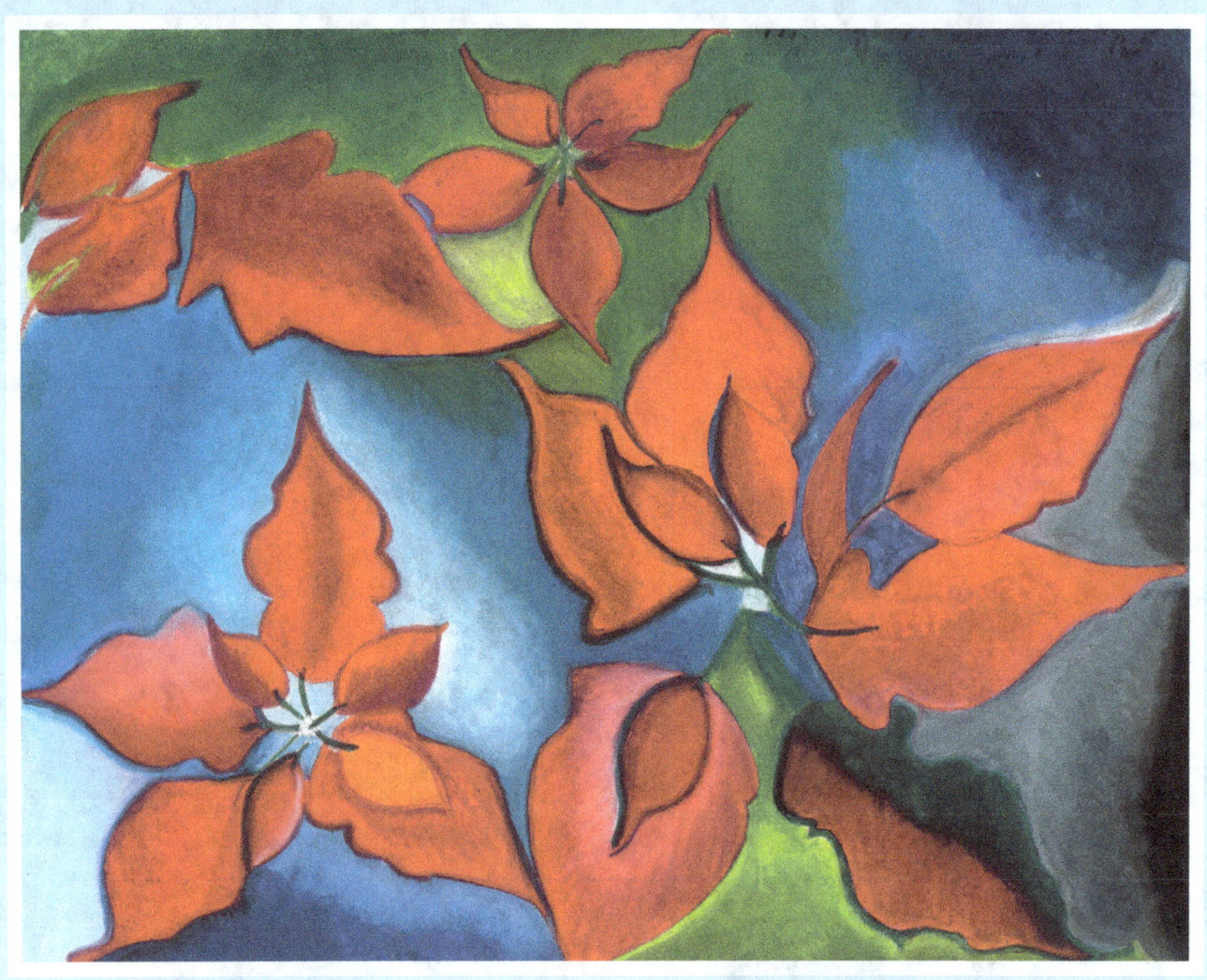

Holiday Blessings

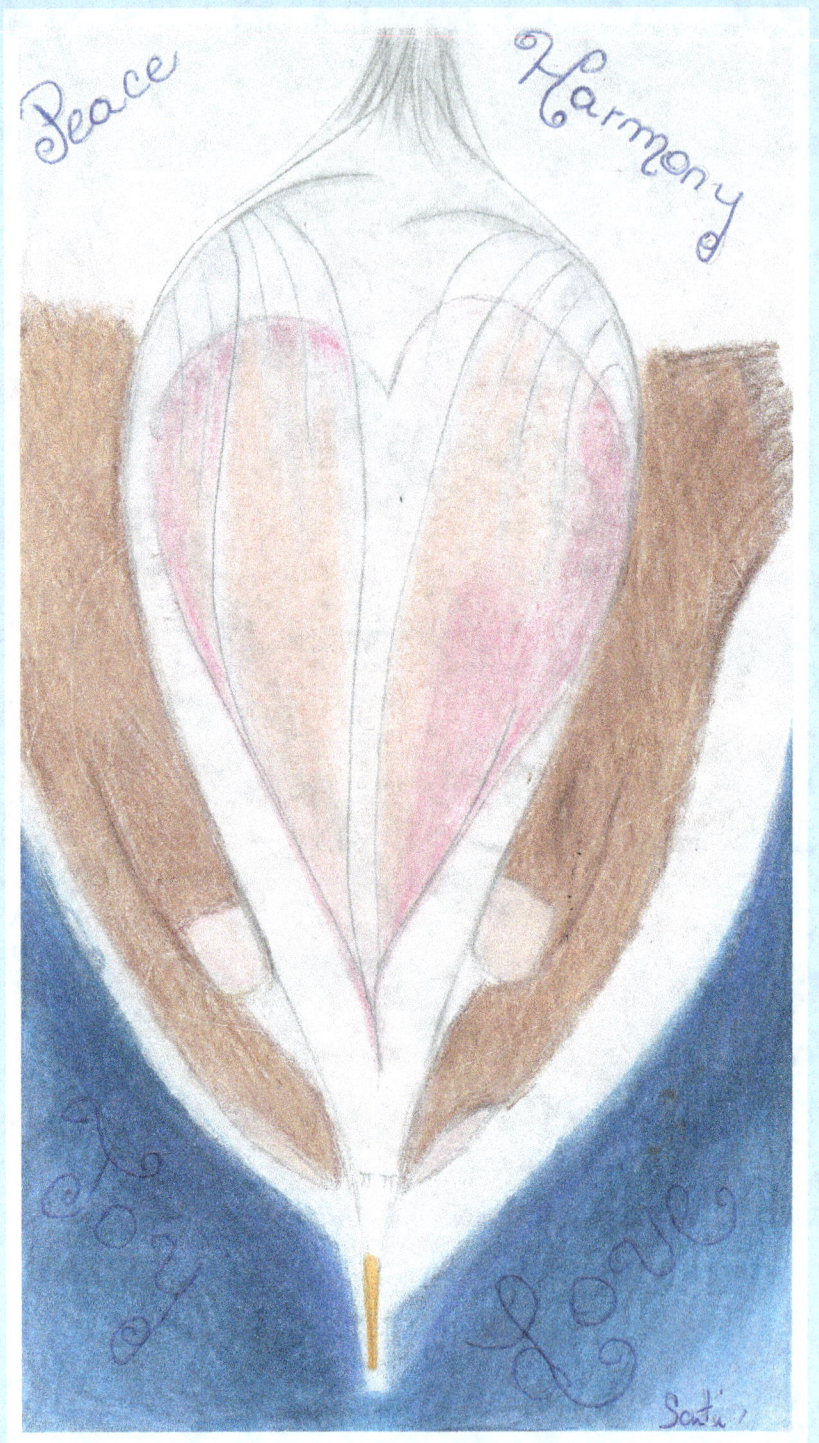

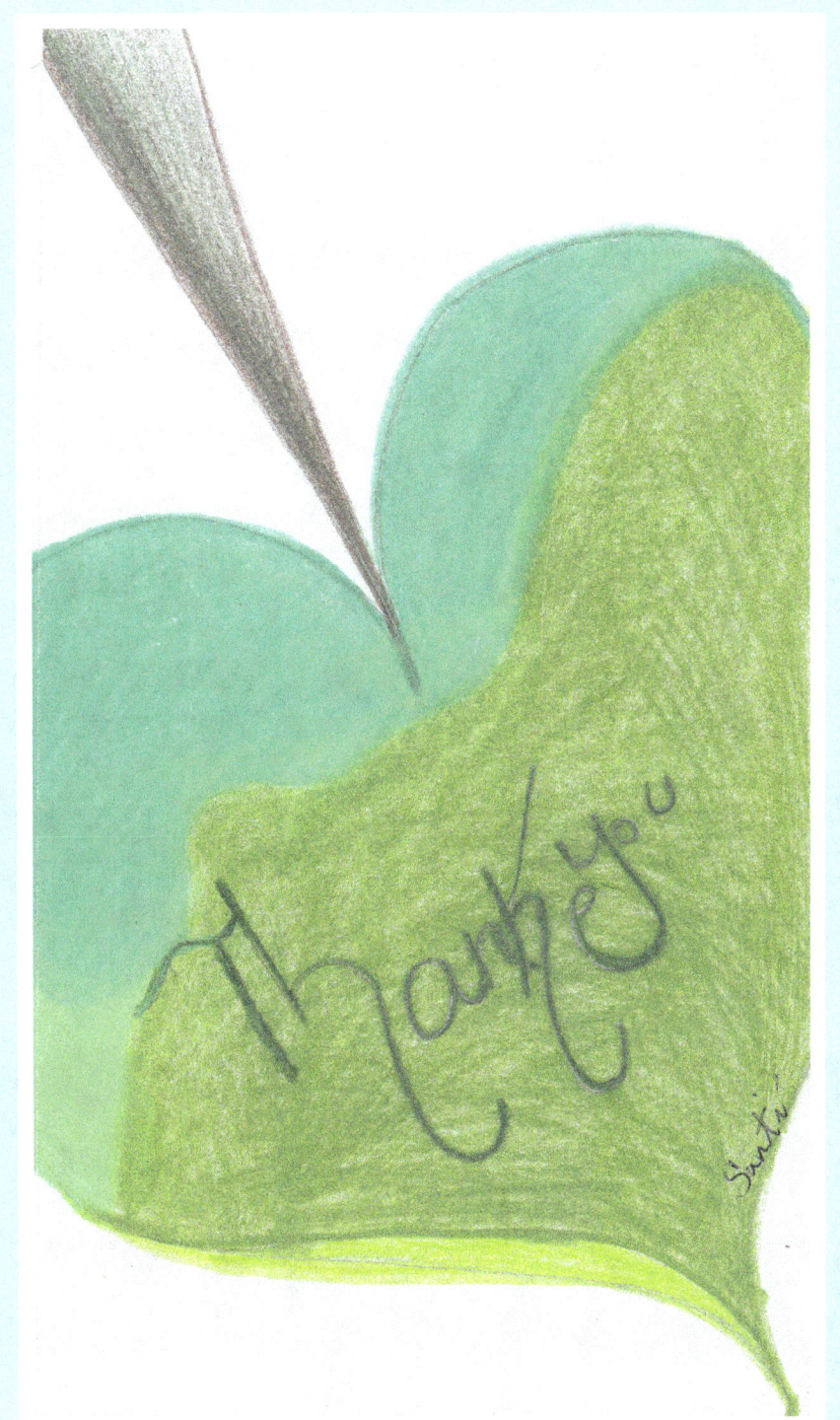

www.ingramcontent.com/pod-product-compliance
Lightning Source LLC
Chambersburg PA
CBHW081308170526
45165CB00010B/3298